THE ULTIMATE
AIR FRYER COOKBOOK

FOR BEGINNERS UK 2023

2000 Days Easy & Affordable Traditional English Air Fryer Recipes For Beginners And Advanced Users

Ewan Cooper

Table of Contents

Introduction

Cooking could get twice more fun and stress-free with that one perfect kitchen appliance! But how? We all know life is not all bed of roses, however, your kitchen experience could be. Cooking is an excellent activity and is very enjoyable when you don't have to wipe out beads of sweat from your forehead every second, and struggle between different appliances all at once.

Certain unique kitchen appliances can make your cooking experience seamless and organize your cooking process. And whether or not you're just setting up your kitchen space or you've established your area, you definitely will find the need for these cooking gems that automatically spur on your cooking creativity and makes a cooking genius out of you.

The air fryer is one of those brilliant kitchen inventions that bring all your cooking into one place and guarantee safe and healthy cooking. The gospel of this appliance has spread worldwide, with believing homeowners singing its praises and its benefits flying across all social media. It is an easy favourite among kitchen enthusiasts because its various features save energy and time and reduce calories.

Thus, what makes using the air fryer better than conventional cooking is the convenience involved and its health benefit, making it almost difficult for it to be a hated piece of appliance. The air fryer uses only little oil to bake, fry and grill, combining the features of about three devices in one compact body with more than 2x effectiveness. Plus, it lets you cook whatever you want at the time and temperature you want, perfectly and healthily.

You could never go wrong with an air fryer, and you must have your first doubts, just like I did; it is actually almost impossible for you not to. My air fryer sat in the corner of my kitchen for months without being used because I thought it was one of those junk you buy because of the hype and isn't that great. Well, you guessed it, after a few times of use, it was evident that this appliance isn't too good to be true, but actually too good and too true.

So, instead of having a deep fryer, an oven and a grilling machine filling up your kitchen space, you could get an air fryer that performs the work of these three perfectly. However, these other appliances have their perks and are most suitable for bigger cooking projects; the air fryer is your kitchen ally for cooking family-sized meals and mini-sized meals, depending on the appliance's capacity.

This book fully exposes all you need to know about the air fryer, the different meals you can make with it and how to unlock your cooking genius by trying out other meals with the air fryer. This book is a cook cheat book for every homemaker, armed with loads of mouth-watering recipes, easily accessible ingredients, and a step-by-step guide on how to cook these meals. You do not have to worry about whether you have years of cooking experience or are just trying out cooking. With these recipes and the air fryer, you're sure to become a genius in no time. Can't wait? Let's dive into it immediately.

RECIPES

Recipe 1:   Air Fried Salmon Cakes

Serving Size: 4

Preparation Time: 10 minutes

Cooking Time: 12 minutes

Ingredients:

- 2 eggs, beaten
- 14 g chopped fresh parsley
- 28 g diced onion
- 1 (418 g.) can salmon

Directions:

1. Combine the salmon, eggs, onion, and parsley in a medium mixing bowl. Divide into 8 groups.
2. Place the salmon cakes in the prepared air fryer basket in a prepared single layer and cook for 6 minutes on each side, or until eventually an instant meat thermometer reads 71 C. Continue with the rest of the salmon cakes.
3. If desired, garnish with parsley and lemon. Have fun while serving!

Recipe 2: Air Fryer Lobster Butter

Serving Size: 4

Preparation Time: 15 minutes

Cooking Time: 15 minutes

Ingredients:

- 2 wedges lemon
- 56 g butter
- 5 ml chopped fresh parsley
- salt and ground black pepper to taste
- 5 ml lemon zest
- 2 (113 ml) lobster tails
- 1 clove garlic, grated

Directions:

1. Preheat the air fryer to a heat of 195 degrees Celsius.
2. Butterfly lobster tails by cutting the hard outer shells and flesh with kitchen shears lengthwise. Cut to the shell bottoms but not through them. Split the tail in half.
3. Oil and heat the pan. Warm the lemon zest and garlic for 30 seconds, or until aromatic.
4. Brush the lobster tails with 28 g of the butter mixture; remove any additional spread butter to avoid infection with raw lobster. Season with pepper and salt.
5. In a preheated air fryer, cook until the lobster meat is opaque.

6. Any residual butter from the skillet should be spooned over the lobster flesh. Garnish with lemon wedges and parsley.

Recipe 3:   Bacon and Peppers Biscuits

Serving Size: 4

Preparation Time: 20 minutes

Cooking Time: 12 minutes

Ingredients:

- 100 gr (3.5 oz) of flour
- 1 small red pepper
- 50 gr (1.7 oz) of softened butter
- 80 gr of grated Parmesan cheese
- 8 slices of bacon
- Salt and pepper to taste

Directions:

1. Cut the butter into chunks and put it in a bowl.
2. Mix the flour and Parmesan.
3. Put the salt, bacon, pepper, and pepper into the dough and knead.
4. After, roll out the dough on a lightly floured surface and form many biscuits.
5. Place the biscuits inside the air fryer and eventually cook at 180 ° C (356 ° F) for 12 minutes.
6. Once cooked, take the biscuits from the air fryer, place them on a serving dish, let them cool and then serve.

Recipe 4: Barbecue Chicken Thighs

Serving Size: 3

Preparation Time: 20 minutes

Cooking Time: 40 minutes

Ingredients:

- 6 chicken thighs with skin on
- 5ml oil
- 14g of plain flour
- 14g of barbecue seasoning

Directions:

1. Spray the chicken thighs with the oil
2. Mix together the flour and seasoning and rub into the chicken thighs
3. Arrange the thighs in your air fryer and cook for 30 minutes turning halfway through
4. Serve with air fryer potato fries or salad.

Recipe 5: Blackberry French Toast

Serving Size: 6

Preparation Time: 10 minutes

Cooking Time: 20 minutes

Ingredients:

- 407 g blackberry jam, warm
- 340 g bread loaf, cubed
- 226 g cream cheese, cubed
- 4 eggs
- 5 ml cinnamon powder
- 450 ml half and half
- 100 g brown sugar
- 5 ml vanilla extract
- Cooking spray

Directions:

1. Cooking spray your air fryer and set it to 148 degrees Celsius.
2. On the bottom, layer blueberry jam, half of the bread cubes, cream cheese, then the remaining bread.
3. Whisk together the sugar, eggs, half and half, cinnamon, and vanilla extract in a large-sized mixing bowl. Pour the bread mix on top.
4. Cook for 20 minutes before dividing amongst plates for breakfast.

Recipe 6: Blue Turkey

Serving Size: 2

Preparation Time: 20 minutes

Cooking Time: 30 minutes

Ingredients:

- 8 slices of ham
- Olive oil to taste
- 100 ml (1 cup) of half and half
- 600 gr (21.1 oz) of turkey breast in one piece
- 100 grams (3.5 oz) of blue cheese
- Salt and pepper to taste
- 1 sprig of rosemary

Directions:

1. Cut the turkey into 4 slices of the same size, season with salt and pepper.
2. Wrap the turkey with the slices of ham and then tie the meat with kitchen string.
3. Wash the sprig of rosemary and divide it into four parts.
4. Put the rosemary between the kitchen string and the turkey meat.
5. Brush the meat with olive oil and then place it in the air fryer basket.
6. If your deep fryer is not big enough, you can cook the fillet in two separate cooks.
7. Cook the fillets at 200°C (392°F) for 6 minutes, then turn the slices. Cook for another 6 minutes.

8. When cooked, remove them from the fryer and wrap them in aluminum foil.

9. Then proceed to prepare the accompanying sauce.

10. Cut the blue cheese into cubes and put it in a saucepan with half and half.

11. Put the saucepan on the stove; cook until the cheese has entirely melted and the sauce has taken on a thick and homogeneous consistency.

12. Remove the turkey breast from the aluminum foil and free it from the kitchen string.

13. Put the turkey slices on serving plates, sprinkle them with the blue cheese sauce and serve.

Recipe 7: Breaded Eggplants

Serving Size: 4

Preparation Time: 15 minutes

Cooking Time: 10 minutes

Ingredients:

- 2 eggplants
- 2 eggs
- 30 ml (2 tbsp) of half and half
- 120 gr (1 cup) of all-purpose flour
- 1 cup of (200 gr) of breadcrumbs
- A pinch of salt and pepper

Directions:

1. First, beat the egg and half and half together in a shallow dish.
2. Mix the breadcrumbs, salt, and pepper on a separate plate.
3. Peel, wash, dry and cut the eggplants into thick slices.
4. Preheat the prepared air fryer for a few minutes at 200 ° C (392°F).
5. Brush the eggplant slices with olive oil.
6. Put the breaded eggplant in the preheated fryer.
7. Cook the breaded eggplant slices for 10 minutes.
8. Turn the eggplant slices after 5 minutes and when ready, serve hot with a favorite sauce.

Recipe 8: Breakfast Pea Tortilla

Serving Size: 8

Preparation Time: 10 minutes

Cooking Time: 7 minutes

Ingredients:

- 454 g baby peas
- 57 g butter
- 367 g yogurt
- 8 eggs
- 13 g mint, chopped
- Salt and black pepper to the taste

Directions:

1. In a pan large enough to fit your air fryer, melt the butter over medium heat, then add the peas, stir, and cook for a few minutes.
2. Meanwhile, in a mixing dish, combine half of the yoghurt, salt, pepper, eggs, and mint.
3. Pour this over the peas, mix, and cook for 7 minutes at 176° C in your air fryer.
4. Spread the remaining yoghurt on top of the tortilla and serve.

Recipe 9: Broccoli Cheddar Chicken Fritters

Serving Size: 8

Preparation Time: 10 minutes

Cooking Time: 10 minutes

Ingredients:

- 454 g boneless skinless chicken thighs, cut into small pieces
- 2 large eggs
- 5 ml garlic powder
- 63 g all-purpose flour
- 235 g shredded cheddar cheese
- 142 g broccoli florets, steamed and chopped fine
- salt & pepper to taste
- Olive oil

Directions:

1. Mix the salt, shredded cheese, almond flour, bite-size chicken pieces, eggs, broccoli, garlic powder, and pepper.
2. Preheat your air fryer to 204° C and cook for 8 minutes.
3. Cook the chicken pieces for 2 minutes on the opposite side.
4. Repeat these steps until you are runs out. Serve and enjoy

Recipe 10: Broccoli Crust Pizza

Serving Size: 4

Preparation Time: 15 minutes

Cooking Time: 12 minutes

Ingredients:

- 340 g riced broccoli, steamed and drained well
- 1 large egg
- 45 g grated vegetarian Parmesan cheese
- 45 ml low-carb Alfredo sauce
- 56 g shredded mozzarella cheese

Directions:

1. Mix egg, broccoli, and Parmesan.
2. Set the air fryer to 187°C set the timer to 5 minutes and cook the crust as you turn.
3. On top, Alfredo sauce and mozzarella cheese. Return the air fryer basket to the prepared air fryer and cook for another 7 minutes, or until the cheese is actually brown and bubbling. Serve immediately.

Recipe 11: Cheesy Bacon Hasselback Chicken

Serving Size: 3

Preparation Time: 10 minutes

Cooking Time: 15 minutes

Ingredients:

- 3 chicken breasts skinless, boneless
- 113 g. cream cheese 1/2 block
- 56 g colby jack cheese shredded
- 56 g pepper jack cheese shredded
- 60 g cheddar cheese shredded
- 56 g cooked bacon chopped
- 30 g spinach fresh, chopped
- 5 ml. garlic minced
- 5 ml. smoked paprika
- 2.5 ml. salt
- 2.5 ml. pepper
- 112 g bocconcini mini mozzarella balls

Directions:

1. Mix all of the remaining ingredients, except the bocconcini.
2. Fill each slit with the cheese mixture, then top with the bocconcini balls.

3. Before placing each chicken breast in the air fryer basket, brush it with olive oil or nonstick cooking spray. Place the basket in your air fryer.
4. Preheat the air fryer to 182°C. Cook for 15 minutes. Serve

Recipe 12: Chicken Burgers with Ham and Cheese

Serving Size: 4

Preparation Time: 12 minutes

Cooking Time: 16 minutes

Ingredients:

- 40 g soft bread crumbs
- 3 tablespoons milk
- 1 egg, beaten
- ½ teaspoon dried thyme
- Pinch salt
- Freshly ground black pepper, to taste
- 570 g chicken mince
- 70 g finely chopped ham
- 75 g grated Gouda cheese
- Olive oil for misting

Directions:

1. Mix milk, salt, thyme, bread crumbs, egg, and pepper. Add the chicken and mix gently but thoroughly with clean hands.
2. Oil and preheat the air fryer and bake for 16 minutes. Serve immediately.

Recipe 13: Chicken Fajitas

Serving Size: 4

Preparation Time: 15 minutes

Cooking Time: 32 minutes

Ingredients:

- 2 sliced peppers (Any colour although the yellow and orange ones tend to be sweeter)
- 1 sliced onion
- 450g of chicken breast meat
- 20g of fajita seasoning. Add more, or less, depending on how spicy you actually like your food (You'll find jars of powdered fajita seasoning in supermarkets and most farm shops)
- 5–10ml of oil

Directions:

1. Slice the chicken into strips of about half a 2cm in width
2. In a bowl, coat the sliced chicken and vegetables with the fajita seasoning and spay with the oil
3. Arrange the mixture into an air fryer bowl or basket
4. Cook for 15–18 minutes. Shake the basket half way through. Check after 15 minutes and if necessary cook for another 5 minutes to crisp up
5. Serve in tortilla wraps with sour cream or guacamole. Alternatively, serve on a bed of rice.

Recipe 14: Chicken Goujons

Serving Size: 4

Preparation Time: 10 minutes

Cooking Time: 15 minutes

Ingredients:

- 500g chicken breast meat
- 60g mayonnaise
- 20g mustard
- 30ml full fat milk
- 40g bacon powder
- 5ml oil

Directions:

1. Line the air fryer tray with foil or parchment and spay with the oil
2. Cut the chicken into 5/6 cm strips – no thicker than 2 cm
3. Mix the mayonnaise, mustard and milk in a bowl
4. Rub the mayonnaise mixture into the goujons and then coat them with the bacon powder
5. Arrange the goujons on the air fryer tray and cook for approximately about 15 minutes turning halfway through
6. Serve and enjoy.

Recipe 15: Chicken Parmesan

Serving Size: 4

Preparation Time: 10 miuntes

Cooking Time: 15 minutes

Ingredients:

- 119 g panko bread crumbs
- 23 g parmesan, grated
- 1 g garlic powder
- 240 g white flour
- 1 egg, whisked
- 680 g chicken cutlets, skinless and boneless
- Salt and black pepper to the taste
- 113 g mozzarella, grated
- 473 ml tomato sauce
- 4 g basil, chopped

Directions:

1. Mix parmesan, panko, and garlic powder.
2. In a separate bowl, combine the prepared flour and the egg.
3. Before immersing the chicken in flour, egg mixture, and panko, season it with salt and pepper.
4. Place the chicken in an air fryer-safe baking dish, fill with tomato sauce, and top with mozzarella. Cook for 7 minutes at 190 degrees C in an air fryer.

5. Distribute among plates, top with basil, and serve.

Recipe 16: Classic Mini Meatloaf

Serving Size: 6

Preparation Time: 10 minutes

Cooking Time: 25 minutes

Ingredients:

- 454 g ground beef
- 1/4 medium yellow onion, peeled and diced
- 1/2 medium green bell pepper, seeded and diced
- 1 large egg
- 21 g blanched finely ground almond flour
- 15 ml Worcestershire sauce
- 2.5 ml garlic powder
- 5 ml dried parsley
- 28 g tomato paste
- 60 ml water
- 15 ml powdered erythritol

Directions:

1. Mix egg, onion, ground beef, pepper, and almond flour. Season with garlic powder and parsley and pour in the Worcestershire sauce. Mix until well combined.
2. Bake in two (4") loaf pans after dividing the batter in half.

3. Mix the water, tomato paste, and erythritol. Each loaf should be topped with half of the mixture.
4. Place bread pans in the air fryer basket in batches as actually needed.
5. Set the temperature of the prepared air fryer to 176°C and the timer for 25 minutes, or until the internal temperature reaches 82°C.
6. Serve immediately.

Recipe 17: Coconut Chicken Bites

Serving Size: 4

Preparation Time: 10 minutes

Cooking Time: 13 minutes

Ingredients:

- 10 ml garlic powder
- 2 eggs
- Salt and black pepper to the taste
- 89 g panko bread crumbs
- 53 g coconut, shredded
- Cooking spray
- 8 chicken tenders

Directions:

1. Mix salt, eggs, garlic powder and pepper.
2. In a separate dish, stir together the coconut and panko.
3. Dip the prepared chicken tenders in the egg mixture and then in the coconut mixture.
4. Spray the chicken bits with cooking spray, place them in the prepared air fryer basket, and cook at 176° C for 10 minutes.
5. Arrange them on a platter to serve as an appetizer.

Recipe 18: Corn with Lime and Cheese

Serving Size: 2

Preparation Time: 10 minutes

Cooking Time: 15 minutes

Ingredients:

- 2 corns on the cob, husks removed
- A drizzle of olive oil
- 83 g feta cheese, grated
- 5 g sweet paprika
- Juice from 2 limes

Directions:

1. Cook at 204 degrees C for 15 minutes, flipping once, after rubbing corn with oil and paprika.
2. Divide corn among plates, cover with cheese, drizzle with lime juice, and serve as a side dish.
3. Enjoy!

Recipe 19: Crackers Breadcrumbs Crispy Lamb Chops

Serving Size: 4

Preparation Time: 10 minutes

Cooking Time: 18 minutes

Ingredients:

- 8 lamb chops
- 200 grams (7 oz) of saltine crackers
- 2 eggs
- 80 ml (1/3 cup) of coconut milk
- Olive oil to taste
- Salt and Pepper to Taste

Directions:

1. Start by washing and drying the lamb chops. Also, remove excess fat and thin them with a meat mallet.
2. Shell the eggs in a bowl. Add the salt, coconut milk, and pepper and beat them with a fork.
3. Put the cutlets inside and let them soften for 30 minutes.
4. In the meantime, take the crackers, put them in the glass of the mixer, and chop them until you get a fairly fine mixture.
5. Now put the chopped crackers on a plate.

6. After 30 minutes, pass the lamb chops over the crackers.

7. Place the ribs in the fryer basket and sprinkle olive oil on the surface.

8. Cook the ribs for 10 minutes at 200 °C (392°F), then turn them, sprinkle them with a bit of oil and continue cooking for another 6/8 minutes.

9. As soon as the chops are ready, remove them from the deep fryer and let them rest for approximately about 5 minutes.

10. Put them on the plates. Serve and enjoy.

Recipe 20: Empanadas

Serving Size: 4

Preparation Time: 10 minutes

Cooking Time: 25 minutes

Ingredients:

- 1 package of empanada shells
- 15 ml olive oil
- 454 g beef meat, ground
- 1 yellow onion, chopped
- Salt and black pepper to the taste
- 2 garlic cloves, minced
- 2.5 ml cumin, ground
- 56 g tomato salsa
- 1 egg yolk whisked with 15 ml water
- 1 green bell pepper, chopped

Directions:

1. Oil and heat the pan, then brown the meat on both sides.
2. After adding the onion, garlic, salt, pepper, bell pepper, and tomato salsa, cook for 15 minutes.
3. Empanada shells should be filled with cooked meat, brushed with egg wash, and sealed.
4. Place them in the air fryer's steamer basket and cook for 10 minutes at 176° C.
5. Arrange on a plate as an appetiser.

Recipe 21: Flavored Rib

Serving Size: 2

Preparation Time: 15 minutes

Cooking Time: 30 minutes

Ingredients:

- Salt and black pepper to the taste
- 30 ml oregano, dried
- 15 ml olive oil

For the rub:

- 15 ml cumin, ground
- 45 ml sweet paprika
- 907 g rib eye steak
- 30 ml onion powder
- 30 ml garlic powder
- 12 g brown sugar
- 15 ml rosemary, dried

Directions:

1. Combine paprika, onion and garlic powder, sugar, oregano, rosemary, salt, pepper, and cumin in a mixing bowl; stir and massage this mixture over the steak.

2. Season with salt and pepper, rub with oil again, and cook at 204° C for 20 minutes, flipping halfway through.
3. Transfer the steak to a chopping board, slice it, and serve with a side salad.

Recipe 22: Gratin Oysters

Serving Size: 4

Preparation Time: 15 minutes

Cooking Time: 10 minutes

Ingredients:

- 16 oysters already opened and cleaned
- 100 g (3.5 oz) of breadcrumbs
- 6 chopped mint leaves
- 4 cherry tomatoes
- Salt and pepper to taste
- Olive oil to taste

Directions:

1. Wash the prepared cherry tomatoes and cut them into cubes.
2. Put the cherry tomatoes in a bowl and add the breadcrumbs, mint, salt, pepper and 4 tablespoons of olive oil. Mix until you get a homogeneous breading.
3. Place the prepared oysters in the air fryer and cover them with the breading.
4. Close the air fryer and cook at 180 ° C (356 ° F) for 10 minutes.
5. Once cooked, take the oysters from the air fryer, place them on serving plates, and serve.

Recipe 23: Ham Breakfast Pie

Serving Size: 6

Preparation Time: 10 minutes

Cooking Time: 25 minutes

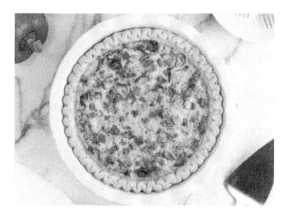

Ingredients:

- 453 g crescent rolls dough
- 2 eggs, whisked
- 470 g cheddar cheese, grated
- 15 g parmesan, grated
- 135 g cooked and chopped
- Salt and black pepper to the taste
- Cooking spray

Directions:

1. Preheat your air fryer to 176°C and coat it with frying spray.
2. Whisk together the eggs, cheddar cheese, parmesan, salt, and pepper in a mixing dish, then pour over the dough.
3. Spread the ham on top, then cut the remaining crescent roll dough into strips and place them on top of the ham. Bake for 25 minutes at 148° C.
4. Breakfast should be served with the pie.

Recipe 24: Leek Mini Quiches

Serving Size: 4

Preparation Time: 15 minutes

Cooking Time: 25 minutes

Ingredients:

- 1 roll of puff pastry
- 20 gr (0.7 oz) of cheddar
- 2 leeks
- 2 whole eggs
- 200 gr (7 oz) of cooking cream
- Nutmeg to taste
- Salt and pepper to taste

Directions:

1. Remove the hardest part from the leeks, wash them, and cut them into rings.
2. Season the leeks with salt, oil, and pepper, and cook at 180 ° C (356 ° F) for 5 minutes.
3. Add the eggs, cooking cream, chopped cheddar and nutmeg and mix well.
4. Roll out the puff pastry. Cut it into small discs of dough.
5. Brush canapes molds with olive oil and put the puff pastry inside.
6. Put the leek mixture on the bottom and put the molds in the air fryer.
7. Cook at 200 ° C (392 ° F) for 20 minutes.
8. After cooking, take the mini quiche out of the air fryer and let them cool.

9. When the quiches have cooled, remove them from the molds, place them on plates and serve.

Recipe 25: Lemon Prawns

Serving Size: 2

Preparation Time: 10 minutes

Cooking Time: 7 minutes

Ingredients:

- 350g uncooked prawns
- 10ml lemon juice
- 1 lemon
- 2g garlic powder
- 15ml oil
- Salt and pepper to season

Directions:

1. Mix all the the ingredients in a bowl
2. Spay the air fryer bowl with the oil
3. Arrange the prawns in the basket and cook for 6–7 minutes shaking the basket every few minutes
4. Lift the prawns out with a spoon and soak up any excess fat with kitchen roll
5. Serve.

Recipe 26: Mac and Cheese

Serving Size: 4

Preparation Time: 10 minutes

Cooking Time: 22 minutes

Ingredients:

- 250g macaroni pasta
- 250g grated cheese
- 650ml milk
- 2 grated garlic cloves
- 10g dried oregano
- Salt and pepper to season

Directions:

1. Mix the ingredients together in a bowl
2. Oil and heat the baking tray. Cook for 18 minutes stirring every 3–4 minutes or continue until cooked
3. Spoon into four bowls to serve and sprinkle with a little more grated cheese or Parmesan
4. Great eaten straight from the bowl with and accompanied by a prepared glass of chilled white wine.

Recipe 27: Marinated Flank Steak

Serving Size: 4

Preparation Time: 5 minutes

Cooking Time: 10 minutes

Ingredients:

- 227 g flank steak
- 63 ml low sodium soy sauce
- 5 ml beef paste or bouillon
- 1/4 Balsamic or Italian dressing
- salt and pepper to taste
- 5.8 grams brown sugar, regular or sugar substitute
- 10 ml garlic paste or 5 ml ground garlic
- 30 ml Worcestershire sauce
- 30 ml chili garlic sauce

Directions:

1. Mix the marinade ingredients in zipper-style bag. Refrigerate the steak in a bag for at least 2 hours.
2. Preheat the air fryer for approximately about 5 minutes at 204 degrees Celsius.
3. On the interior surface or grill insert, apply nonstick oil spray.
4. Cook the steak for 4 minutes on one side. Cook for 3 minutes more, then check with a meat thermometer. Cook for a further 5 minutes if required.

5. Set aside the steak for 5-10 minutes to enable the fluids to redistribute. Cut against the grain to serve.

Recipe 28: Marinated Pork Chops and Onions

Serving Size: 6

Preparation Time: 24 hours

Cooking Time: 25 minutes

Ingredients:

- 2 pork chops
- 60 ml olive oil
- 2 yellow onions, sliced
- 2 garlic cloves, minced
- 10 g mustard
- 5 ml sweet paprika
- Salt and black pepper to the taste
- 2.5 ml oregano, dried
- 2.5 ml thyme, dried
- A pinch of cayenne pepper

Directions:

1. In a mixing bowl, combine the oil, garlic, mustard, paprika, black pepper, oregano, thyme, and cayenne.
2. Toss the onions with the meat and mustard mixture to coat, then cover and chill for 1 day.
3. Cook the beef and onion combination in an air fryer pan for 25 minutes at 182 degrees C.
4. Serve everything on separate plates.

Recipe 29: Mushroom Quiche

Serving Size: 4

Preparation Time: 10 minutes

Cooking Time: 10 minutes

Ingredients:

- 17 ml flour
- 14 g butter, soft
- 9 inch pie dough
- 2 button mushrooms, chopped
- 37 g ham, chopped
- 3 eggs
- 1 small yellow onion, chopped
- 76 g heavy cream
- A pinch of nutmeg, ground
- Salt and black pepper to the taste
- 2.5 ml thyme, dried
- 56 g Swiss cheese, grated

Directions:

1. Flour your actual work surface and roll out the pie dough.
2. Press it into the bottom of your air fryer's pie plate.
3. Whisk together the butter, mushrooms, ham, onion, eggs, heavy cream, salt, pepper, thyme, and nutmeg in a mixing bowl.
4. Spread this over the pie shell, then top with Swiss cheese and set in the air fryer.

5. Cook your quiche for 10 minutes at 204 degrees C.
6. Serve.

Recipe 30: Peas Meatballs

Serving Size: 2

Preparation Time: 25 minutes

Cooking Time: 20 minutes

Ingredients:

- 100 gr (3.5 oz) of already boiled peas
- 2 eggs
- 60 gr (1/4 cup) of grated cheddar cheese
- Milk to taste
- 300 gr (10.5 oz) of minced pork
- Breadcrumbs to taste
- Olive oil to taste
- Salt and pepper to taste

Directions:

1. Put the minced pork, an egg, cheddar cheese, salt and pepper into a bowl.
2. Mix the ingredients with a fork.
3. Now add the boiled peas and a bit of breadcrumbs. Mix first with a fork and then knead everything with your hands.
4. If the dough is soft, add a few more breadcrumbs. Instead, if it is too dry, add a few tablespoons of milk.
5. Moisten your hands with water and start forming the meatballs.
6. They must be about the size of a walnut.

7. Beat the other egg and put some breadcrumbs on a plate. First, put the meatballs in the egg and then eventually roll them in breadcrumbs.
8. Place the pork meatballs well apart in the basket of the air fryer.
9. Sprinkle each meatball with olive oil, and set the fryer at 200° (392°F) for 5 minutes.
10. After 5 minutes, turn the meatballs, sprinkle a bit of oil, and cook for another 2-3 minutes.
11. Serve still hot with a favorite sauce.

Recipe 31: Roast Pork Loin

Serving Size: 6

Preparation Time: 30 minutes

Cooking Time: 1 hour 40 minutes

Ingredients:

- 1kg pork loin joint with the rind on
- 4g sea salt
- 2 grated garlic cloves
- 4g dried mixed herbs
- 5ml oil

Directions:

1. Score the rind with a sharp knife making 3–4 deep cuts
2. Mix the salt, garlic and mixed herbs and rub the mixture into the pork rind making sure to fill the scored sections
3. Spray the pork with the oil
4. Place the joint in the prepared air fryer basket and cook for 50 minutes (or 25 minutes per 450g) shaking the basket every 10 minutes. Check the meat is cooked with a meat thermometer – it should be at least 65 degrees
5. Remover the pork from the fryer and rest for 10 minutes
6. Serve with apple sauce and air fryer roast potatoes.

Recipe 32: Roasted Tomatoes with Basil

Serving Size: 2

Preparation Time: 10 minutes

Cooking Time: 10 minutes

Ingredients:

- 4 medium tomatoes
- 8 cherry tomatoes
- 4g dried basil
- Salt and pepper to season
- 5–10ml oil

Directions:

1. Slice the larger tomatoes in half
2. Leave the cherry tomatoes whole
3. Sprinkle half the basil and seasoning over the tomatoes and spray with oil then turn them and sprinkle the rest of the seasoning and oil
4. Arrange in the air fryer basket and cook for 10 minutes turning halfway through
5. Serve as a side with steak or salmon.

Recipe 33: Rosemary Roasted Vegetables

Serving Size: 6

Preparation Time: 10 minutes

Cooking Time: 20 minutes

Ingredients:

- 1 yellow pepper
- 1 red pepper
- 1 courgette
- 1 onion
- 1 broccoli head
- 1 teaspoon of dried rosemary
- Salt and pepper to season
- 10ml oil

Directions:

1. Slice or cube the vegetables but don't have pieces more than 2 cm thick
2. Wash, pat dry, and separate the broccoli into individual florets
3. Toss the vegetables in the dried rosemary and the oil
4. Season to your taste
5. Cook for in the air fryer for 20 minutes. Shake the basket half way through.
6. Serve.

Recipe 34: Salami and Blue Cheese Potatoes

Serving Size: 4

Preparation Time: 10 minutes

Cooking Time: 10 minutes

Ingredients:

- 4 large potatoes
- 8 salami slices
- 80 gr (1/3 cup) of blue cheese
- 12 almonds
- salt pepper to taste

Directions:

1. Drain the boiled potatoes and let them cool.
2. Cut them in two lengthwise and gently empty them with a spoon or digger.
3. Put the potatoes in a bowl, and mash them with a fork to reduce them to a puree.
4. Add salt and pepper, salami and softened blue cheese.
5. Add the crumbled almonds and mix to mix all the ingredients well.
6. Fill the potato boats with that filling.
7. Place the potatoes directly on the basket of the air fryer and cook them at 200 °F (392°f) for about 10 minutes until they are golden brown.
8. Serve the potatoes still hot.

Recipe 35: Salami and Peas Turkey Meatloaf

Serving Size: 4

Preparation Time: 10 minutes

Cooking Time: 25 minutes

Ingredients:

- 600 gr (3 cups) of ground turkey breast
- 100 gr (1 cup) of salami
- 60 gr (1/4 cup) of grated cheddar cheese
- 2 eggs
- 200 gr (7 oz) of boiled peas
- 2 spring onions
- 1 carrot
- 100 ml (half a glass) of Cognac
- 1 sprig of chopped parsley
- Breadcrumbs to taste
- Salt and pepper to taste
- Olive oil to taste

Directions:

1. Start by finely chopping the salami with a knife.
2. Remove the green part of the spring onions, wash the white part, and cut it into thin slices.

3. Put the spring onions, salami, turkey meat and 100 grams (1 cup) of peas in a bowl.
4. Stir with a fork and as soon as they are well blended, add the eggs, cheddar cheese, 3 tbsp of breadcrumbs, chopped parsley, salt and pepper.
5. Knead well and as soon as you have obtained a homogeneous mixture, form the meatloaf with your hands and then pass it on to the breadcrumbs.
6. Peel and wash the carrot and then cut it into cubes.
7. Take a disposable pan suitable for your fryer and brush it with a little oil.
8. Put the carrot, the remaining peas, and the chopped parsley at the bottom of the pan.
9. Season them with pepper and salt, and mix to flavor them well.
10. Now place the meatloaf on top and sprinkle everything with Cognac.
11. Cook the meatloaf at 200 °C (392°F) for 10 minutes. Turn it over and eventually continue cooking for another 10/15 minutes, sprinkling it with the cooking juices and adding a little water if necessary.
12. Cut it into slices, put it on plates and sprinkle it with the vegetables and cooking juices.
13. You can serve.

Recipe 36: Salmon Tartlets

Serving Size: 3

Preparation Time: 20 minutes

Cooking Time: 15 minutes

Ingredients:

- 1 roll of puff pastry
- 300 gr (10.5 oz) of smoked salmon
- 100 g (3.5 oz) of Greek yogurt
- 2 sprigs of dill
- 1 lemon
- Chopped chives to taste
- Salt and pepper to taste

Directions:

1. Wash the dill, chop it, and put it in a bowl.
2. Chop the salmon and put it in the bowl with the dill.
3. Add the grated lemon zest, pepper, salt, and Greek yogurt and mix well.
4. Brush 4 tartlet molds with olive oil and put the puff pastry inside.
5. Fill the tartlets with the salmon filling and place the molds in the air fryer.
6. Cook at 180 ° C (356 ° F) for 15 minutes.
7. When the tartlets are cooked, remove them from the prepared air fryer and let them cool.

8. Once cold, remove the tartlets from the molds, place them on serving plates, sprinkle them with chopped chives and serve.

Recipe 37: Shrimp Muffins

Serving Size: 6

Preparation Time: 10 minutes

Cooking Time: 26 minutes

Ingredients:

- 1 spaghetti squash, peeled and halved
- 28 g mayonnaise
- 28 g mozzarella, shredded
- 227 g shrimp, peeled, cooked, and chopped
- 126 g cups panko
- 5 ml parsley flakes
- 1 garlic clove, minced
- Salt and black pepper to the taste
- Cooking spray

Directions:

1. Cook squash halves in an air fryer for 16 minutes at 176°C, then leave aside to cool and scrape flesh into a basin.
2. Combine the salt, pepper, parsley flakes, panko, shrimp, mayo, and mozzarella in a mixing bowl.
3. Spray a muffin pan that fits your air fryer with cooking spray and spoon the squash and shrimp mixture into each cup.
4. Cook for 10 minutes at 182 degrees Celsius in your air fryer.
5. Serve the muffins on a platter as a snack.

Recipe 38: Smoked Cheese and Bacon Pork Meatloaf

Serving Size: 4

Preparation Time: 10 minutes

Cooking Time: 25 minutes

Ingredients:

- 400 gr (2 cups) of ground pork meat
- 200 gr (1 cup) of smoked cheese
- 60 ml (1/4 cup) of half and half
- 100 grams (3.5 oz) of smoked bacon
- 1 tsp of chopped sage
- ½ tsp of nutmeg
- Olive oil to taste
- Salt and pepper to taste

Directions:

1. Start with preparing the meat. Put the minced pork meat in a bowl, half and half, chopped bacon, diced smoked cheese, a pinch of nutmeg, chopped sage, salt and pepper.
2. Moisten your hands and form the meatloaf.
3. Take a large aluminum foil to hold the meatloaf and grease it with oil.
4. Arrange the pork meatloaf inside the aluminum foil and then close everything.

5. Place the packet inside the fryer basket and set it at 200 °C (392°F) for 20 minutes.
6. When the time has elapsed, check the cooking. If it still does not seem cooked enough, continue to cook for another 5 minutes with the aluminum foil open.
7. Remove the meatloaf from the fryer, let it cool, and cut it into slices.

Recipe 39: Spicy Chicken Wings

Serving Size: 4

Preparation Time: 13 minutes

Cooking Time: 30 minutes

Ingredients:

- 1kg chicken wings
- 14g of garam masala seasoning
- 5–10ml oil

Directions:

1. Trim off the actual tips of the chicken wings using scissors
2. Coat the wings in the oil and seasoning
3. Arrange in the air fryer and cook for 20–25 minutes shaking the basket every 5 minutes
4. When they are cooked the meat should easily come away from the bone
5. Remove from the fryer and serve immediately while still crisp
6. Serve with any dip of your choice – maybe sour cream or a cucumber raita.

Recipe 40: Spinach Nuggets

Serving Size: 2

Preparation Time: 15 minutes

Cooking Time: 30 minutes

Ingredients:

- 200 gr (1 cup) of spinach (already boiled and drained)
- 60 gr (1/4 cup) of grated cheddar cheese
- 2 big eggs
- 500 gr chicken breast (17.5 oz)
- Olive oil to taste
- Breadcrumbs to taste
- Salt to taste

Directions:

1. First, boil the cleaned and sliced chicken breast in a pan or saucepan, covering it with water.
2. Add salt and finish cooking.
3. Boil the spinach or let it defrost if you are using frozen ones.
4. Let them drain well: this step is very important to prevent the dough from being too watery and soft.
5. Blend the spinach and then the chicken in a blender, reducing them to puree.
6. Combine the spinach, chicken, eggs, cheddar and salt in a bowl.

7. Shape into nuggets by dividing the dough into equal parts and pressing them so that they take shape.

8. After forming the spinach, pass them into the breadcrumbs.

9. Place them and sprinkle them with olive oil on the air fryer previously heated to 200 ° C (392°F) and cook for about 10 minutes, turning them halfway through cooking, until golden brown.

10. Serve still hot.

Recipe 41: Spinach, Bacon, and Cheddar Omelette

Serving Size: 8
Preparation Time: 10 minutes
Cooking Time: 10 minutes

Ingredients:

- 8 eggs
- Olive oil to taste
- 150 gr (5.2 oz) of boiled spinach
- Salt and pepper to taste
- 100 gr (3.5 oz) of smoked bacon
- 150 gr (5.2 oz) of cheddar

Directions:

1. Cut the bacon into cubes. Brush a baking pan with olive oil and put the bacon and the spinach inside.
2. Cook at 180 ° C (356 ° F) for 3 minutes.
3. Meanwhile, break the prepared eggs into a bowl, add the prepared salt and pepper and the diced cheddar, and mix well with a fork.
4. After 3 minutes, pour the prepared egg mixture over the spinach and bacon and continue cooking for another 7 minutes.
5. After cooking, take the baking pan from the fryer and fold the omelette into two parts.
6. Cut the omelette into slices, place them on serving plates and serve.

Recipe 42: Spinach Balls

Serving Size: 6

Preparation Time: 10 minutes

Cooking Time: 7 minutes

Ingredients:

- 57 g butter, melted
- 2 eggs
- 250 g flour
- 454 g spinach
- 50 g feta cheese, crumbled
- 1.25 ml g nutmeg, ground
- 30 g parmesan, grated
- Salt and black pepper to the taste
- 15 ml onion powder
- 15 g whipping cream
- 5 ml garlic powder

Directions:

1. In a blender, combine the spinach, butter, eggs, flour, feta cheese, parmesan, nutmeg, whipped cream, salt, pepper, onion, and garlic pepper until smooth. Place for 10 minutes in the freezer.
2. Cook for 7 minutes at 149° C.
3. During a party, serve as an appetizer.

Recipe 43: Stuffed Peppers

Serving Size: 2

Preparation Time: 10 minutes

Cooking Time: 15 minutes

Ingredients:

- 4 green peppers
- 450g lean minced beef
- 50g finely chopped spring onion
- 60g grated mozzarella
- 250g cooked rice
- 250ml readymade tomato and basil sauce (Most supermarkets have fresh sauces in the chilled aisle. One of these is perfect for this recipe)
- 2 grated garlic cloves
- 2g dried sage
- 2g dried basil
- 15ml olive oil
- 5ml oil
- Salt and pepper to season

Directions:

1. Fry the mince in a little oil until browned
2. Drain the meat and return to the pan
3. Stir in the spring onion, sage, basil, oil and seasoning and mix well

4. Add the tomato and basil sauce and cooked rice
5. Stir until the ingredients are evenly blended
6. Cut the tops off the prepared peppers and scoop out the seeds
7. Stuff each pepper with an equal amount of the mixture
8. Spray some oil around the inside of the air fryer basket and line with parchment, making holes so that the hot air can circulate
9. Arrange the peppers in the basket and cook for 10 minutes
10. Open the fryer and add the grated mozzarella and cook for 5 more minutes
11. Serve with a glass of chilled white wine.

Recipe 44: Stuffed Tomatoes with Spinach and Cheese

Serving Size: 4

Preparation Time: 20 minutes

Cooking Time: 15 minutes

Ingredients:

- 4 Tomatoes ripe beefsteak
- 4 ml Ground Black Pepper
- 2.5 ml Kosher Salt
- 284 g Frozen Spinach thawed and squeezed dry
- 147 g garlic-and-herb Boursin cheese
- 45 ml sour cream
- 45 g Grated Parmesan Cheese finely grated

Directions:

1. Remove the tomatoes' tops. Using a small spoon, remove and discard the pulp.
2. Season the insides of the tomatoes with 2.5 mL black pepper and 1.25 mL salt. While you prepare the filling, drain the tomatoes on paper towels.
3. Mix the sour cream, Boursin cheese, spinach, salt and pepper, and 45 g of the grated parmesan. Stir until all of the ingredients are well combined. Divide the mixture evenly among the tomatoes.
4. Finally, sprinkle with the remaining 45 g grated parmesan.

5. Half-fill the air fryer basket with tomatoes. In the air fryer, heat the filling for 15 minutes at 176°C.

Recipe 45: Tender Air Fryer Steak with Garlic Mushrooms

Serving Size: 2

Preparation Time: 5 minutes

Cooking Time: 15 minutes

Ingredients:

- 15 ml avocado oil
- 454 g ribeye steaks
- 473 g halved fresh mushrooms
- 2.5 ml salt
- 2.5 ml black pepper
- 28 g unsalted butter (melted)
- 3 cloves minced garlic
- 1.25 g red pepper flakes (optional)
- chopped parsley (optional garnish)

Directions:

1. Pat the steaks dry before cutting them into 1/2" cubes. In a large mixing bowl, combine the steak cubes.

2. In a large mixing bowl, combine the cubed steak and cut fresh mushrooms in half.

3. In a large mixing bowl, combine the steak chunks and mushrooms with the melted butter, garlic, salt, pepper, and red pepper flakes.

4. Place the mixture in an air fryer basket in an even, non-overlapping layer. (Depending on your AirFryer model, you may need to cook in batches.)

5. The steak and mushrooms were air fried for 7-15 minutes, turning twice throughout that period. Check the steak after 7 minutes to see whether it's done to your liking. If it's still too pink, keep cooking.

6. Garnish with parsley and serve immediately for the best flavor and texture.

Recipe 46: Tomato and Basil Tart

Serving Size: 2

Preparation Time: 10 minutes

Cooking Time: 14 minutes

Ingredients:

- 1 bunch basil, chopped
- 4 eggs
- 1 garlic clove, minced
- Salt and black pepper to the taste
- 114 g cherry tomatoes, halved
- 60 g cheddar cheese, grated

Directions:

1. In a mixing bowl, combine the eggs, salt, black pepper, cheese, and basil.
2. Pour mixture into a baking dish that fits your air fryer, cover with tomatoes, and cook for 14 minutes at 160 degrees C.
3. After slicing, serve immediately.

Recipe 47: Trout with Potatoes and Cherry Tomatoes

Serving Size: 4

Preparation Time: 15 minutes

Cooking Time: 20 minutes

Ingredients:

- 4 trout fillets of 250 gr (8.8 oz) each
- 600 gr (21 oz) of potatoes
- 1 red onion
- 300 gr (10.5 oz) of tomatoes
- 1 lemon
- Salt and pepper to taste
- Olive oil to taste

Directions:

1. Wash the trout fillets and remove the bones.
2. Peel the prepared potatoes, wash them, and cut them into cubes.
3. Peel the prepared onion and cut it into slices.
4. Wash the tomatoes and cut them into slices.
5. Brush a baking pan and put the potatoes, tomatoes, and onion on the bottom.
6. Add oil, salt and pepper, and then put the trout fillets on top.

7. Season the trout with oil, salt, pepper, and lemon juice, and put the baking pan in the air fryer.
8. Cook at 200 ° (392 ° F) for 20 minutes, turning the trout after 10 minutes.
9. When the trout is cooked, take it out of the prepared air fryer and place it on the plates.
10. Add the potatoes, onion and tomatoes, and serve.

Recipe 48: Tuna Fish Cakes

Serving Size: 4

Preparation Time: 10 minutes

Cooking Time: 10 minutes

Ingredients:

- 140g tinned, drained tuna
- 60g bacon powder
- 5g dried herbs
- 110g grated cheese
- 7g mayonnaise
- 1 beaten egg
- 10ml water
- 10ml oil

Directions:

1. Preheat your air fryer to 190 degrees
2. Mix all the prepared ingredients except the oil together in a bowl (It's best to actually use your hands for this)
3. Make 8 equally sized fish cakes and spray with the oil
4. Arrange the fish cakes in the fryer basket (It's probably best to do these in 2 batches unless you have a large fryer)
5. Cook for 8 minutes shaking the bowl halfway through
6. Serve with air fryer potato fries or salad.

Recipe 49: Turkey Burrito

Serving Size: 2

Preparation Time: 10 minutes

Cooking Time: 10 minutes

Ingredients:

- 4 slices turkey breast already cooked
- ½ red bell pepper, sliced
- 2 eggs
- 1 small avocado, peeled, pitted and sliced
- 36 g salsa
- Salt and black pepper to the taste
- 225 g mozzarella cheese, grated
- Tortillas for serving

Directions:

1. In a mixing bowl, whisk the eggs with salt and pepper to taste, then pour them into a pan and set it in the air fryer basket.
2. Cook for 5 minutes at 204°C before removing pan from fryer and placing eggs on a platter.
3. Distribute the eggs, turkey meat, bell pepper, cheese, salsa, and avocado among the tortillas on a work surface.
4. Roll your burritos and lay them in an air fryer coated with tin foil.
5. Heat the burritos for 3 minutes at 149° C before dividing them onto plates and serving.

Recipe 50: Vegan Avocado Wraps

Serving Size: 4

Preparation Time: 10 minutes

Cooking Time: 5 minutes

Ingredients:

- 8 vegan egg-roll wrappers
- 3 mashed avocados
- ½ tin of chopped tomatoes
- 5ml oil
- Salt and pepper to season

Directions:

1. Preheat your air fryer to 180 degrees
2. Mix the ingredients together in a bowl
3. Lay out the egg-roll wrappers and fill each one, folding corner to corner and then wrapping, sealing the sides with water
4. Spray the wraps with 10ml oil
5. Arrange in the air fryer basket and cook for 5 minutes until crispy shaking the bowl halfway through
6. Serve with a prepared dipping sauce of your choice.

Printed in Great Britain
by Amazon

14161234R00045